THE SEARCH FOR
OLinguito

DISCOVERING A NEW SPECIES

SANDRA MARKLE

MILLBROOK PRESS / MINNEAPOLIS

For dear friends Pam and Dwain Kitchens

The author would like to thank the following people for sharing their enthusiasm and expertise: Dr. Robert Anderson, City College of New York; Dr. Kristofer Helgen, Curator of Mammals for the Smithsonian Institution's National Museum of Natural History; Dr. Clinton Jenkins, SavingSpecies; Dr. Roland Kays, Head of Biodiversity Research Lab, North Carolina Museum of Natural Sciences and North Carolina State University; and Dr. C. Miguel Pinto, American Museum of Natural History, Department of Mammalogy.

Millbrook Press™
An imprint of Lerner Publishing Group, Inc.
241 First Avenue North
Minneapolis, MN 55401 USA

For reading levels and more information, look up this title at www.lernerbooks.com.

Main body text set in Adrianna Regular.
Typeface provided by Chank.

Library of Congress Cataloging-in-Publication Data

Names: Markle, Sandra, author.
Title: The search for Olinguito : Discovering a new species / Sandra Markle.
Description: Minneapolis : Millbrook Press, [2017] | Audience: Ages 6–10. | Audience: K to grade 3. | Includes bibliographical references.
Identifiers: LCCN 2016010446 (print) | LCCN 2016011665 (ebook) | ISBN 9781512410150 (lb : alk. paper) | ISBN 9781512428421 (eb pdf)
Subjects: LCSH: Procyonidae—Juvenile literature. | Rare mammals—South America—Juvenile literature. | Cloud forest animals—Juvenile literature.
Classification: LCC QL737.C26 M367 2017 (print) | LCC QL737.C26 (ebook) | DDC 599.76/3—dc23

LC record available at https://lccn.loc.gov/2016010446

Manufactured in the United States of America
2-52430-21262-2/28/2022

TABLE OF CONTENTS

Big News! • 4

What in the World? • 6

Different or New? • 14

The Long, Wide Search • 20

Meet the Olinguito • 34

Author's Note • 37

Be a Science Detective! • 38

Source Notes • 38

Glossary • 39

Find Out More • 39

Index • 40

Big news!

On August 15, 2013, reporters from around the world gathered in an auditorium at the Smithsonian National Museum of Natural History, in Washington, DC. Excitement filled the air. Kristofer Helgen was about to announce a rare discovery. He and several other scientists had found a new animal, called an olinguito (oh-ling-GHEE-toe). Among the group of mammals it belonged to, it was the first new species discovered in thirty-five years.

Finding the olinguito had required more than ten years of scientific detective work in museums, zoos, and mountain forests. It had all started when Kristofer went to work to solve a little mystery about another mammal, an olingo (oh-LING-goh). But how did this mystery lead to the olinguito?

No one knew it at the time, but the search for the olinguito would be a huge adventure.

Kristofer Helgen shares a photo of an olinguito in August 2013.

WHaT iN THe WORLD?

Kristofer Helgen was curious. A scientist at the Smithsonian National Museum of Natural History, he is in charge of the museum's collection of mammals (warm-blooded animals with hair, whose babies are born alive and nursed on mother's milk). In 2002 scientists were debating questions

Olingos live up among tree branches and eat mostly fruit.

about the olingo species. This mammal, related to raccoons, lives in Central America and South America. Some experts thought all olingos belonged to one species. Others believed that certain olingos from different regions were different enough from one another to be unique species. Kristofer wanted to find out which was true.

Animals are considered distinct species if they are so different from one another that they are unlikely to mate and produce babies. If olingos did include more than one species, Kristofer wondered, just how many olingo species existed?

Kristofer works at the Smithsonian National Museum of Natural History, home to a number of stuffed olingos.

He didn't have to go far to start his research. For more than one hundred years, researchers had been exploring olingos' home forests. They had brought back the pelts (preserved skins with fur) and skulls of some of the animals they encountered, including olingos. These were carefully stored in museums. So when Kristofer began studying olingos, he examined olingo pelts and skulls at the Smithsonian. These gave him a close-up look without having to chase after live animals in the wild.

To see more examples, Kristofer visited other museums around the world. When he visited the Chicago Field Museum in Illinois, he had already been investigating olingos for a year. He had become very familiar with olingo features. He had determined that there were, in fact, several species of olingo, with minor differences among them.

But when he opened one drawer of olingo pelts, he was shocked. Several were more reddish orange than any olingo pelts he'd studied. The fur was also longer and softer. The ears were smaller and fuzzier. And the tails on each of these pelts was shorter than usual for any kind of olingo he knew of. These differences stood out from other, smaller variations among olingo species.

Kristofer got goose bumps. "Those pelts weren't like anything I'd ever seen before in an olingo," he said. "I wasn't sure they were olingos at all."

The orange fur of some pelts caught Kristofer's eye. All other olingo pelts he'd seen were brown.

Kristofer then found the skulls of the animals whose pelts were in that museum drawer. He compared those to skulls from several olingo species. The skulls from the animals with the odd pelts looked very different. They were rounder, and the muzzle (nose and mouth) on each was less pointy.

Kristofer used digital calipers, a tool for precise measuring, to check the teeth in those skulls. They were larger and pointier than any olingo teeth he'd seen.

Different fur. Different skull shape. Different teeth!

Kristofer thought what he'd found was too different to be yet another species of olingo. He wondered, "Could it be that right here in these drawers is a species . . . that all other zoologists [scientists who study animals] have overlooked?"

This animal's skull and teeth set it apart from olingo skulls. An animal's teeth are a clue to what it eats. Sharp, pointy teeth are usually used to tear meat, while wider, flatter teeth grind plants, nuts, and seeds.

These pelts are stuffed to show an animal's size and shape.

MEET THE RACCOON FAMILY

Animals are classified (grouped together) into families by features they have in common. Members of the raccoon family (known to scientists as Procyonidae) are small, usually with slender bodies and long tails. Many have banded (striped) tails and facial markings. Check out what sets each animal apart.

RACCOON

SIZE: Up to 37 inches (93 centimeters) long with a tail nearly body length. It weighs as much as 20 pounds (9 kilograms).

DISTRIBUTION: North America, Central America, and South America

CHARACTERISTICS: It is mainly active at night and often lives alone. It eats small animals such as frogs and insects, and fruit—often picking up food with its front feet.

COATIS

SIZE: Up to 27 inches (69 cm) long with an equally long tail. It weighs as much as 18 pounds (8 kg).

DISTRIBUTION: North America, Central America, and South America

CHARACTERISTICS: It lives in groups in treetops and is mainly active during the day. It has a long, bendable nose that it can push into tight places to find insects, lizards, and snakes. It also eats fruit.

KINKAJOU

SIZE: Up to 22 inches (56 cm) long with an equally long tail. It weighs as much as 7 pounds (3 kg).

DISTRIBUTION: Central America and South America

CHARACTERISTICS: It has a long prehensile (gripping) tail. It lives in groups and is active at night. It has a long, skinny tongue that it pushes out to slurp honey from beehives and pull termites out of their mounds.

CACOMISTLE

SIZE: Up to 19 inches (47 cm) long with a tail slightly longer than its body. It weighs about 2 pounds (1 kg).

DISTRIBUTION: Mexico through Panama

CHARACTERISTICS: It is active at night. It eats fruit, insects, and small animals.

RINGTAIL

SIZE: Up to 17 inches (42 cm) long with a tail slightly longer than its body. It weighs about 3 pounds (1.4 kg).

DISTRIBUTION: North American deserts

CHARACTERISTICS: It can rotate its hind feet 180 degrees to run up and down trees. Its claws are straight and semi-retractable. It is active at night and usually feeds alone, eating fruit, insects, and small animals.

OLINGO

SIZE: Up to 17 inches (42 cm) long with a tail slightly longer than its body. It weighs about 3 pounds (1.4 kg).

DISTRIBUTION: Central America and South America

CHARACTERISTICS: It has small ears and a flattened head. Its hind legs are longer than its front legs. Active at night, it feeds alone and eats mainly fruit. It is able to produce a foul smell if alarmed.

Different or new?

Were the pelts and skulls stored with the olingos really from a new species?

Kristofer searched for other preserved samples that were like the pelts he had found in Chicago. He didn't have to look very long. He found a pelt and skull with the same features at the American Museum of Natural History in New York City. The pelt was labeled #66753. The number led to information about where and when the animal had been collected. In this case, the pelt was from the 1923 Anthony-Tate Expeditions, when Harold Anthony and George Tate explored the rugged mountain forests of Ecuador.

Those explorers had labeled the animal as a kinkajou, another raccoon relative. Later, someone moved #66753 to the olingo drawer at the museum. However, it was exactly like the samples in Chicago. And pelt #66753 was in great condition. Kristofer thought it could be a holotype, a single preserved sample used to describe and name a brand-new species. That is, *if* what he'd found was a brand-new species. Was it?

Kristofer needed to do two things to find out.

During a six-month trek, the team of explorers on the Anthony-Tate Expeditions in Ecuador *(above)* collected fifteen hundred specimens (individual plants or animals), including #66753.

The expedition note about #66753 *(top)*, made in the field at the time it was collected, tells that the animal was thought to be a kinkajou.

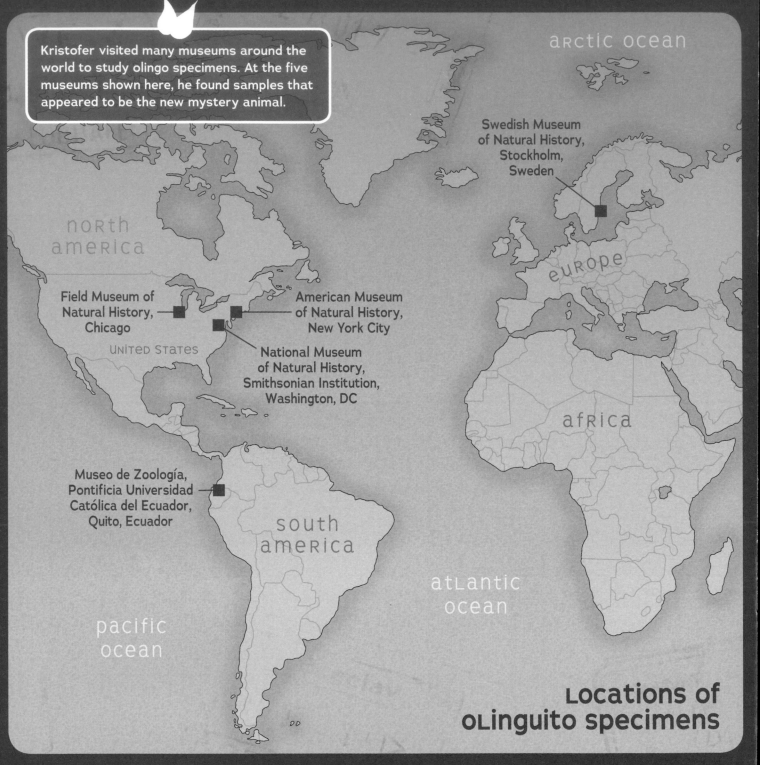

Kristofer visited many museums around the world to study olingo specimens. At the five museums shown here, he found samples that appeared to be the new mystery animal.

arctic ocean

Swedish Museum of Natural History, Stockholm, Sweden

north america

Field Museum of Natural History, Chicago

UNITED STATES

American Museum of Natural History, New York City

National Museum of Natural History, Smithsonian Institution, Washington, DC

europe

africa

Museo de Zoología, Pontificia Universidad Católica del Ecuador, Quito, Ecuador

south america

atlantic ocean

pacific ocean

LOCATIONS of oLinguito specimens

First, Kristofer needed to find even more preserved samples with the same features as #66753. That would prove these few weren't just oddball olingos. So over the next couple of years, he continued to visit museums around the world. He was still investigating the number of different species of olingos. But he also kept searching for more samples like #66753.

Before Kristofer's olingo study was complete, he had visited seventy-five museums. And he had discovered more samples of the mystery animal. One was in Sweden at the Swedish Museum of Natural History. Several more were at the American Museum of Natural History in New York and the Museo de Zoología in Ecuador.

Discovering those samples still wasn't enough proof, though, that he had found a distinct, new species and not just another type of olingo. For that, Kristofer needed to look at their DNA (deoxyribonucleic acid)—the substance in plant and animal cells that carries genetic information.

Kristofer needed to confirm that the DNA of #66753 didn't match olingo DNA. All mammals share similar DNA, but the more distantly related two animals are, the more different their DNA is. Animals from distinct species are likely to have DNA so different that even if the animals mated, they probably couldn't produce babies. If they did, their offspring would likely be unable to reproduce.

Kristofer first examined olingo DNA. He collected olingo tissue samples from living zoo animals as well as from frozen, preserved olingo tissue.

A tissue sample is spun to separate the DNA from the rest of the tissue.

Since his research had identified several different species of olingo, he needed to test tissue samples from each. Once those DNA tests were completed, scientists had a map of the typical genetic makeup (DNA patterns) of each olingo species.

By 2005 it was time for the next step, testing the DNA from #66753. Tissue was taken from the skull bones of #66753 and from several other samples with those same features. Then this genetic makeup was carefully compared to each of the olingo species. The results were clear: sample #66753 was not an olingo.

Kristofer really had discovered a new member of the raccoon family—a brand-new kind of animal. He called it an olinguito, Spanish for "little olingo."

Of course, Kristofer then had another big question to answer. Were there any olinguitos still alive in the wild?

The features of this skull, #32609, matched #66753. It is from another olinguito.

The Long, Wide Search

Before confirming that #66753 was a new species, Kristofer had heard a curious story. In the late 1960s, Ivo and Inga Poglayen-Neuwall were in charge of a special mammal exhibit at the Louisville Zoo in Louisville, Kentucky. This couple made it their goal to exhibit every living species of the raccoon family, including olingos. They also hoped to launch a breeding population of olingos. They brought in a female olingo from Colombia and named her Ringerl. However, when they housed her with male olingos, she refused to choose a mate. Eventually, they sold her to another zoo.

Kristofer contacted Inga, who had long since retired, to find out more about Ringerl. There was always something different about Ringerl, Inga told him. At the time, her keepers just thought she was fussy. Later, though, she also refused to take a mate at the Salt Lake City Zoo—and then at the Tucson Zoo, the Bronx Zoo, and the National Zoo in Washington, DC. Although Ringerl lived until 1976, she never produced babies.

Ringerl's story made Kristofer curious. Was it possible she never mated with an olingo because she wasn't one? He obtained a frozen sample of Ringerl's blood and tissue that was stored at the National Institutes of Health database in Bethesda, Maryland. A DNA test of this material proved he was right. Ringerl was not an olingo. In fact, her DNA nearly matched that of #66753. She was an olinguito.

This was exciting news. It meant olinguitos were alive in the 1970s. But Kristofer was searching for these animals about thirty years later. If any were still living, where could they be?

This is Ringerl. She was moved from zoo to zoo because her keepers kept hoping that somewhere she'd choose an olingo mate.

21

Kristofer wanted to search for olinguitos in the wild. But where should he look? He knew just whom to ask. His friend Roland Kays was head of the Biodiversity Research Lab at the North Carolina Museum of Natural Sciences. Roland was the world's leading expert on wild olingo behavior. He was excited to learn about Kristofer's discovery of the olinguito.

And Roland knew where they should begin. "I couldn't wait to search for living olinguitos," he said. "It made sense to start in the kind of habitat [environment] where Ringerl was found." That meant a high-up forest habitat in South America— the cloud forest.

Roland Kays studies an olingo in Panama.

22

WHAT IS A CLOUD FOREST?

A cloud forest is also called a tropical montane forest. It grows on high mountains where the air is moist and cool—but not cold and snowy. Only about 1 percent of all forest area around the world is cloud forest. This unusual habitat is found in Central and South America, the Caribbean, East and central Africa, Indonesia, Malaysia, the Philippines, and Papua New Guinea.

Cloud forests are rich with life. They're perfect for many kinds of trees, including those that produce fruit such as figs. Ferns, mosses, and orchids also grow well on trees in the foggy atmosphere. In addition, these forests are home to many uncommon animals, such as golden toads, green-throated mountain gem hummingbirds, howler monkeys, spectacled bears, and olingos.

Kristofer and Roland hoped they'd be able to add olinguitos to that list.

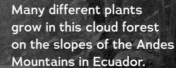

Many different plants grow in this cloud forest on the slopes of the Andes Mountains in Ecuador.

Although South America's cloud forest habitat is limited, it still covers huge areas. Kristofer and Roland needed a way to narrow the search for an olinguito. Soon they got a lucky break.

A scientist friend of Kristofer and Roland at the Smithsonian had an intern from Ecuador named Miguel Pinto. Miguel was interested in surveying the different kinds of mammals in his home country. And Ecuador was a promising place to look for olinguitos, since the Anthony-Tate Expeditions had collected #66753 there in 1923. So Miguel traveled to Ecuador to scout a site for an olinguito search.

The scientists gave Miguel a video camera to film the forest area he thought was the best possible site for an expedition. "I already had contacts in Ecuador and had some forest places in mind," Miguel said. "I was excited to be helping organize an expedition to search for a brand-new kind of animal."

Miguel Pinto explores an area of cloud forest in Ecuador.

Check out the olinguito's claws. They're perfect for climbing tall trees.

In June 2006, Miguel went to Ecuador. He visited several forests but found the trails very rugged—too difficult for an expedition team hauling scientific equipment to travel. Then he visited the Otonga Cloud Forest Reserve. He had helped with fieldwork there during high school, and he knew the reserve caretaker. Miguel talked to him about what animals he'd seen in the reserve.

The caretaker reported seeing kinkajous, olingos, and owl monkeys. He didn't recall seeing anything that fit the olinguito's description. But the caretaker also told him, "Who knows what else moves around in the treetops at night? If you aim a light there, you only see shining eyes."

In the light of the camera flash, an olingo's eyes shine against the dark branches at night.

To have a look for himself, Miguel hiked into the Otonga reserve at night with his camera. He was pleased the trail was much easier to follow than trails in the other forests. After just five minutes of hiking, he heard noises like high-pitched squeaky squeeze toys. When he looked up, the dim moonlight was enough for him to see furry animals with long tails jumping through the tree branches above his head. These animals had bodies similar to olingos, but they didn't quite look like any olingos he'd seen. He aimed the camera and shot a quick video—just in case his suspicions were right and this was the mystery animal.

CARIBBEAN SEA

ATLANTIC OCEAN

VENEZUELA

Otonga Cloud Forest Reserve

COLOMBIA

○★ Quito

pacific ocean

ecuador

BRAZIL

PERU

Cloud forest habitat

● Confirmed olinguito sighting

0   200 Miles

0   200 Kilometers

OLINGUITOS IN SOUTH AMERICA

This map shows where cloud forests stretch across narrow parts of South America. After Miguel first spotted an olinguito in Ecuador, the animals have been seen in several other areas as well.

When Miguel returned to the Smithsonian, that dark footage excited the scientists. "It was a grainy, blurry video," Roland said, "but the animal jumped around the way olingos do. Only the body shape and size was different, which made me think it was an olinguito. It was enough to start me packing."

Kristofer and Roland were eager to see for themselves if the animal caught on film was the same species as the olinguito brought to the Louisville Zoo so many years earlier. The Smithsonian funded a three-week expedition to search for the olinguito.

Kristofer and Roland put together a team of scientists to explore the forest with them. To make the most of this expedition, they would collect information about a wide variety of mammal life in that forest, including olingos and bats.

With this plan in place, they flew to Quito, Ecuador. Then they rented a vehicle to get to the Otonga reserve. Finally, they hired mules to carry their equipment up the mountain trails. They went to a campsite in the cloud forest.

As the last daylight faded, Kristofer and Roland walked through the forest with their team. They aimed flashlights up into the treetops to look for shining eyes—a clue something was there.

At first, they didn't find anything. Sometimes the patches of fog in the forest were so thick that the scientists could barely make out tree branches. Roland remembered thinking, "If olinguitos are mostly active at night, and they live in this mist, it's no wonder this animal has remained hidden for so long."

At the airport, Roland Kays *(above)* looks forward to searching for a living olinguito.

Kristofer *(left)* and another member of his team get their first look at the Otonga reserve.

Just then, a breeze blew. The mist thinned. And when the scientists aimed their lights up into the trees, there it was: a living version of the museum specimens they'd studied. *It was a real live olinguito.*

Before anyone could snap a photo, the animal jumped from branch to branch and was gone. Roland and Kristofer were stunned. They had finally seen an olinguito—but they would have to prove what they'd discovered. They set out to learn more about the mysterious treetop dwellers.

An olinguito looks back at the scientists from the misty treetops.

The scientists needed help from technology to capture photos of the olinguitos. The team set up camera traps in the area where they'd spotted the first one. A camera trap isn't actually a trap but rather a battery-powered camera with a motion sensor. When it detects movement, the camera snaps a picture. The initial placement of the cameras didn't produce any photos. But when the team moved the cameras to other locations, they were able to catch the olinguito in action.

Roland finishes attaching a camera trap where olinguitos are likely to climb down.

Later in 2006, after the expedition, Kristofer and Roland wrote a report about discovering the olinguito. They submitted it to a scholarly journal for publication to share the news. A number of experts checked the report, and it was rejected. The journal said more information was needed about the olinguito's physical traits and its behavior.

So over the next few years, while Kristofer went on with his olingo research, Roland and Miguel returned to the Otonga reserve and visited other cloud forests in Ecuador and Colombia. They watched more olinguitos in the treetops and began to learn how they live. From 2006 through 2011, other scientists from around the world observed olinguitos too. They even found a baby to study.

The scientists hoped to answer many questions about this species. For example, how do olinguitos find food and shelter? When do they have babies? How do they care for their young? How different is this animal from others in the raccoon family? Slowly, the scientists pieced together key discoveries and began to understand the olinguito's life.

They learned that olinguitos build a nest for sleeping during the day. The nest is often in a hole in a tree or among thick, leafy vines. Olinguitos carry in woolly plant material to make a bed. An adult usually nests alone, using a nest for a couple of days and then moving on.

Near the center of this photo, an olinguito nest is hiding among the high-up branches and leafy vines.

Wherever they are, olinguitos sleep all day and start coming out of their nests as the sun sets. They're active at night, feeding and traveling. Sometimes they move through the trees alone, other times in small groups.

Olinguitos are great climbers and jumpers, using their long tails for balance. The tail can also serve as a blanket when they curl up to sleep.

As treetop dwellers, olinguitos rarely come down. They feed on fruit in the same trees as kinkajous. But the two species don't fight with each other for food. That's because they usually feed at different times of the day.

A mother olinguito, the scientists learned, has only one baby at a time, usually in February or March. The baby stays in the tree nest for about a month. When the cub leaves the nest, the mother carries it on her back until it can walk and climb.

Kristofer, Roland, and their team were thrilled with how much information they had learned about this new species. Solving the mystery of the olinguito had taken a long time and a lot of work. Finally, it was time to share this discovery!

This baby olinguito is about the size of a kitten, small enough to be held in one hand for its photo.

Meet the Olinguito

Kristofer and Roland wrote another report that included all the new information about the olinguito. The report was published in the August 15, 2013, issue of the journal *ZooKeys*. That day Kristofer also officially announced the olinguito to the world at a press conference.

That was more than ten years after he found the olinguito pelts in the Field Museum and seven years after his team first found a living olinguito in the cloud forest. All that time was needed for his team to study the olinguito and then to have other scientists review their research. This peer-review process ensures that new scientific information is reliable.

The olinguito species was added to the mammal group called Carnivora. Because of its claws, skull shape, and the shape of its teeth, it was placed in the same family as raccoons, a smaller group within Carnivora.

Kristofer first announced the olinguito at the Smithsonian National Museum of Natural History in Washington, DC.

Of course, the olinguito wasn't new to the people living near its cloud forest home. Locals had long heard its noises and had even nicknamed it the night monkey. But since it's active at night, few people may have ever caught more than glimpses of it. And for those who'd seen one high up in the branches, it was easily mistaken for an olingo or kinkajou.

With its official announcement, the rest of the world knew about this animal too. Kristofer had the honor of choosing its scientific name. He called it *Bassaricyon neblina*. *Bassaricyon* is part of the scientific name of the olingo. But *neblina* is just for the olinguito. It's Spanish for "foggy mist," describing the cloud forest habitat. "Getting a scientific name out there is fun," Kristofer remarked. "Almost like naming a baby."

An olinguito makes its way across branches in the treetops.

News about the olinguito's discovery spread around the world. People were excited to learn about this cute animal. Even more importantly, interest in the olinguitos started to raise awareness of cloud forests. Since the 1920s, cloud forests in South America had been cleared to make way for farms and coffee plantations. By the time the olinguito became known, nearly half of Ecuador's original cloud forest area was gone.

An organization called SavingSpecies is leading the way to protect what remains of these critical forests in Ecuador and Colombia. This effort will help all the other animals—and plants—that live in this unique environment.

The dusky starfrontlet hummingbird is found only in cloud forests.

And Kristofer Helgen continues to search for what the scientific world has yet to find. Certainly, there are still species around the globe known only to local people. "The discovery of the olinguito reminds us that the world is not yet completely explored," Kristofer said. "Finding the olinguito makes us think—what else is out there?"

The spectacled bear prefers the cloud forests of the Andes Mountains.

AUTHOR'S NOTE

In 2013 I read with amazement the announcement of the olinguito, a newly discovered mammal. I knew at once that the discovery was a story I had to share. Tracking down Kristofer Helgen and Roland Kays was a challenge. These modern-day scientist-explorers are often trekking in wildly remote places. When I did finally have an opportunity to talk to them and hear about the search for a real, live olinguito, I was fascinated.

During Kristofer's search, he was clearly never going to give up. He told of tracking one clue to the next as this mystery unfolded. It was like listening to the plot of an adventure-packed movie.

It was this excitement about solving a mystery—this blend of *Indiana Jones* and scientific investigation—that captured me. And that was what I wanted to infuse into the scientific mystery unfolding in this book. Of course, part of the fun of this story is that the olinguito had been hiding in plain sight for so long. People living near its cloud forest habitat had heard it—possibly even caught a glimpse of it. And even zoologists in the United States had thought Ringerl was simply another olingo.

For me, this scientific mystery is inspiring because it's proof that some of nature's mysteries remain unsolved. With wonder, investigation, creative thinking, and determination, people can still bring fresh discoveries to the world. And along the way, there are sure to be great adventures!

Be a Science Detective!

- *The Search for Olinguito* is all about the scientific search for an animal most of the world didn't know about. But to people who lived near its home environment, the olinguito wasn't strange or new. Only they didn't call it an olinguito. In fact, there were several local names for it, such as one that translates to "night monkey." Can you think of a time you shared something local that was familiar to you but new to a visitor?

- After reading this story, why do you think even the people living near the cloud forest didn't know much about the olinguito's life?

- At the beginning of the chapter "What in the World?," what was Kristofer looking for? How does that change throughout the book and why?

- Kristofer put together a team to help him find a living olinguito. Why was this better than trying to do it alone?

- Have you ever been the one to solve a mystery? What was your favorite part about doing that?

Source Notes

8   Kristofer Helgen, phone call with author, April 6, 2015.

10   Ibid.

22   Roland Kays, phone call with author, March 23, 2015.

24   Miguel Pinto, phone call with author, September 21, 2015.

26   Ibid.

28   Kays, phone call with author, August 5, 2015.

29   Kays, phone call with author, January 6, 2016.

35   Helgen, phone call with author, January 14, 2016.

36   Helgen, phone call with author, March 14, 2016.

LERNER
SOURCE

Expand learning beyond the printed book. Download free, complementary educational resources for this book from our website, www.lerneresource.com.

Glossary

cloud forest: a high mountain forest where the air is usually cool and moist and clouds often hang at treetop level

DNA (deoxyribonucleic acid): the substance in plant and animal cells that carries genetic information, as a set of distinct genes. The order and arrangement of those genes is unique for each species and each individual.

expedition: a journey made for the purpose of exploring or researching

habitat: a living thing's natural home environment

holotype: a single preserved sample that can be used to describe and name a species

mammal: a warm-blooded animal with hair whose babies are usually born alive and nursed on mother's milk

mate: either animal in a pair that breeds together

pelt: preserved skin with fur

skull: the set of bones that forms an animal's head and face

species: a group of similar living things able to mate and produce babies that can also reproduce when they grow up

tissue: a group of cells that forms a structural part of an animal or plant, such as muscle, bone, or leaf

Find Out More

Collard, Sneed B., III. *The Forest in the Clouds*. Watertown, MA: Charlesbridge, 2000.
See how plants, animals, and the unique environment are connected in this look at another cloud forest, the Monteverde Cloud Forest in Costa Rica.

Monteverde Cloud Forest Reserve
http://www.anywherecostarica.com/attractions/reserve/monteverde-cloud-forest
Scroll through the slide show tour of this cloud forest. Don't miss the animal photos to see some of the amazing wildlife living there.

Montgomery, Sy. *Quest for the Tree Kangaroo: An Expedition to the Cloud Forest of New Guinea.* Boston: Houghton Mifflin, 2006. Explore the cloud forest in Papua New Guinea as a team of scientists searches for and studies rare tree kangaroos.

Weird Animals of the Andean Cloud Forests—Wild South America—BBC
https://www.youtube.com/watch?v=PBrStxuOJbs
Watch this short video for a look at some cloud forest animals.

Index

Anthony-Tate Expeditions, 14–15, 24

cacomistles, 13
Carnivora, 34
Chicago Field Museum, 8, 14, 16, 34
cloud forest, 22, 23, 24–31, 34–36
coatis, 12
Colombia, 20, 27, 31, 36

DNA (deoxyribonucleic acid), 17–19, 21

Ecuador, 14–17, 23, 24, 26–28, 31, 36

Helgen, Kristofer, 20–24, 36
    announcement of olinguito, 4–5, 34–35
    discovery of olinguito species, 6–11, 14–19

finding wild olinguitos, 28–33
holotype, 14–15

Kays, Roland, 22–24, 28–33, 34
kinkajou, 13, 14–15, 26, 33, 35

National Institutes of Health database, 21

olingo, 4, 6–8, 20, 35
    characteristics, 13, 28
    habitat, 22, 23, 26
    number of species, 7, 17–19
    pelts and skulls, 8–11
olinguito (*Bassaricyon neblina*), 4–5, 16, 19, 21–33, 34–36
Otonga Cloud Forest Reserve, 26–31

pelt, 8–10, 14, 34
Pinto, Miguel, 24–28, 31
Poglayen-Neuwall, Inga, 20
Poglayen-Neuwall, Ivo, 20

raccoon family, 7, 12–13, 14, 19, 20, 34
Ringerl, 20–22
ringtail, 13

SavingSpecies, 36
scientific journals, 31, 34
#66753, 14–19, 20–21, 24
skull, 8–11, 14, 19, 34
Smithsonian National Museum of Natural History, 4, 6–8, 16, 28, 34

zoologist, 10

Photo Acknowledgments

The images in this book are used with the permission of: © Lavrentyeva/Shutterstock.com (leaf design throughout); © Mark Gurney for Smithsonian/Getty Images, p. 1; © Alex Wong/Getty Images, pp. 5, 19; © Michael and Patricia Fogden/Minden Pictures, p. 6; Courstey of Kristofer M. Helgen, Ph.D., pp. 7, 9, 29; © Saul Loeb/AFP/Getty Images, pp. 10, 11; © Konrad Wothe/Minden Pictures, p. 12 (top); © Pete Oxford/Minden Pictures, p. 12 (bottom); © Michael and Patricia Fogden/Minden Pictures, p. 13 (top); © Gerard Lacz/Minden Pictures, p. 13 (top middle); © Michael Durham/Minden Pictures, p. 13 (third from top); © Rod Williams/Minden Pictures, p. 13 (bottom); Courtesy of: American Museum of Natural History, p. 15 (all); © Laura Westlund/Independent Picture Service, pp. 16, 27; csp_kadmy/fotosearch.com, p. 18; © Poglayen-Neuwall for Smithsonian/Getty Images, p. 21; Courtesy of Roland Kays, pp. 22, 26, 29 (inset); © Image Source/Getty Images, p. 23; Courtesy Miguel Pinto, p. 24; © Tui De Roy/Minden Pictures, pp. 25, 35; © Luis A. Mazariegos, pp. 30, 32, 33, 36 (top); © David Price, Courtesy of Smithsonian Institution, p. 31; AP Photo/Charles Dharapak, p. 34; © Pete Oxford/Minden Pictures, p. 36 (bottom).

Front cover: © Roy Mangersnes/Nature PL/Alamy; © Lavrentyeva/Shutterstock.com (leaf design).